TONS OF FUN

TONS OF FUN

COMPILED BY
JOANNA COLE & STEPHANIE CALMENSON
ILLUSTRATED BY *ALAN TIEGREEN*

Featuring four popular activity books:

**The Eentsy, Weentsy Spider:
Fingerplays and Action Rhymes**

**Why Did the Chicken Cross the Road?
And Other Riddles Old and New**

Six Sick Sheep: 101 Tongue Twisters

Pat-a-Cake and Other Play Rhymes

A BEECH TREE PAPERBACK BOOK
NEW YORK

10 9 8 7 6 5 4 3 2 1
First one-volume Beech Tree edition, 1996
ISBN 0-688-15210-4

CONTENTS

Carlson

THE EENTSY, WEENTSY SPIDER

THE EENTSY, WEENTSY SPIDER

FINGERPLAYS AND ACTION RHYMES

COMPILED BY

JOANNA COLE

AND

STEPHANIE CALMENSON

ILLUSTRATED BY

ALAN TIEGREEN

CONTENTS

FINGERPLAYS AND ACTION RHYMES

Fingerplays and action rhymes, like nursery rhymes, have been kept alive for generations because children love them. The musical language of the rhymes makes them easy to say and remember. The actions, too, are perfect for children, who love to participate. It's fun to make the tickly little steps of "The Eentsy, Weentsy Spider" climbing up the waterspout, to pretend to pound in a nail while singing "The Hammer Song," and to tip over your whole body for "I'm a Little Teapot."

Many of the rhymes reflect a child's world. They are about mealtime and bedtime and families. They are about the natural phenomena a child sees every day—rain, flowers, animals large and small. And they give children an opportunity to learn about left and right, up and down, and their bodies from head to toe.

So say them, sing them—there are musical arrangements at the back of the book—act them out. They really are fun!

TEN LITTLE FIREFIGHTERS

Ten little firefighters
Sleeping in a row.

Ding, ding goes the bell,

And down the pole they go.

Off on the engine, oh, oh, oh.

Using the big hose, so, so, so.

When all the fire's out, home so slow.

Back into bed, all in a row.

BALLOONS

This is the way
We blow our balloon.

Blow!

Blow!

Blow!

This is the way
We break our balloon.

Oh, oh, no!

 # TWO FAT SAUSAGES

Two fat sausages

Sizzling in the pan.

Pop!

One went POP!

The other went BAM!

 # SIX LITTLE DUCKS

Six little ducks
That I once knew.

WIGGLE
FINGERS

Fat ducks, skinny ducks,
Fair ducks, too.

But the one little duck
With a feather on his back,

He led the others with
A quack, quack, quack.

Down to the river
They would go,
Wibble-wobble, wibble-wobble,
To and fro.

But the one little duck
With a feather on his back,

He led the others with a quack, quack, quack!
Quack, quack, quack. Quack, quack, quack.
He led the others with a quack, quack, quack!

OPEN, SHUT THEM

Open,
Shut them.

Open,
Shut them.

Give a little clap.

Open,
Shut them.

Open,
Shut them.

Place them in your lap.

Creep them, creep them.
Creep them, creep them

Right up to your chin.
Open wide your little mouth,

But do not let them in.

RAIN

Pitter-pat, pitter-pat,
The rain goes on for hours.
And though it keeps me in the house,

Drum
fingers
on
floor

It's very   good for   flowers.

APPLES

Way up high in the apple tree,

Two little apples smiled at me.

shake arms

I shook that tree as hard as I could.

Drop hands to lap

Down came the apples—
Mmm, were they good!

TEN LITTLE FINGERS

I have ten little fingers,
And they all belong to me.
I can make them do things.
Would you like to see?

I can shut them up tight

Or open them wide.

I can put them together

Or make them all hide.

I can make them jump high

Or make them go low.

I can fold them up quietly
And sit just so.

THE QUIET MOUSE

Once there lived a quiet mouse | In a quiet little house.
When all was quiet as can be,

OUT POPPED HE!

GRANDMA'S SPECTACLES

Here are Grandma's spectacles,

And here is Grandma's hat;

And here's the way she folds her hands
And puts them in her lap.

I'M A LITTLE TEAPOT

I'm a little teapot,
Short and stout.

Here is my handle.

Here is my spout.

When I get all steamed up,
Hear me shout,
"Tip me over and pour me out!"

 # HERE'S A CUP

Here's a cup,

And here's a cup,

And here's a pot of tea.

Pour a cup,

And pour a cup,

And have a drink with me.

BLUEBIRDS

Two little bluebirds
Sitting on a hill,

One named Jack,

The other named Jill.

Fly away, Jack.

Fly away, Jill.

Come back, Jack.

Come back, Jill.

GREAT BIG BALL

A great big ball,

A middle-sized ball,

A little ball I see.

Let's count them all together—
One,

Two,

Three!

MY HAT

My hat it has three corners,

Three corners has my hat.

If it did not have three corners,

It would not be my hat.

THE EENTSY, WEENTSY SPIDER

ARMS GO UP AS FINGERS "CLIMB"

The eentsy, weentsy spider
Climbed up the waterspout.

Down came the rain

And washed the spider out.

Out came the sun

And dried up all the rain.

And the eentsy, weentsy spider
Climbed up the spout again.

UP TO THE CEILING

Up to the ceiling,

Down to the floor.

Left to the window,

Right to the door.

This is my right hand—
Raise it up high.

This is my left hand—
Reach for the sky.

Twirl hands

Right hand, left hand,
Twirl them around.

Left hand, right hand,
Pound, pound, pound.

 # HERE IS THE CHURCH

Here is the church.

Here is the steeple.

Open the doors

And see all the people.

HERE ARE MOTHER'S KNIVES AND FORKS

Here are Mother's knives and forks.

Here is Grandma's table.

Here is Sister's looking glass,

Rock Cradle

And here is Baby's cradle.

THE HAMMER SONG

Jenny works with one hammer,
One hammer, one hammer.
Jenny works with one hammer.
Then she works with two.

Jenny works with two hammers,
Two hammers, two hammers.
Jenny works with two hammers.
Then she works with three.

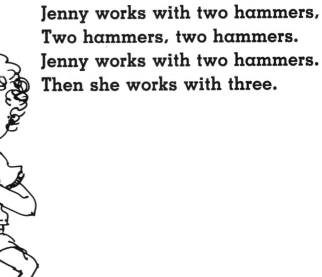

Jenny works with three hammers,
Three hammers, three hammers.
Jenny works with three hammers.
Then she works with four.

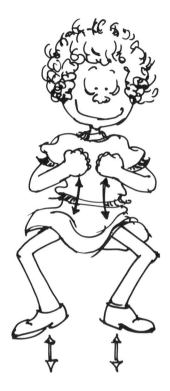

Move head

Jenny works with four hammers,
Four hammers, four hammers.
Jenny works with four hammers.
Then she works with five.

Jenny works with five hammers,
Five hammers, five hammers.
Jenny works with five hammers . . .

Then she goes to sleep!

 **MY TURTLE**

This is my turtle.
He lives in a shell.
He likes his home very well.

He pokes his head out
When he wants to eat.

And he pulls it back
When he wants to sleep.

 # FIVE LITTLE KITTENS

Five little kittens
Standing in a row,

They nod their heads
To the children, so.

They run to the left,
They run to the right,

They stand up and stretch
In the bright sunlight.

Along comes a dog,
Who's in for some fun.

Meow! See those
Five kittens run.

– 33 –

THE WHEELS ON THE BUS

The wheels on the bus
Go round and round,
Round and round,
Round and round.
The wheels on the bus
Go round and round
All over town!

Twirl
hands

The driver on the bus
Goes "Move to the rear!
Move to the rear!
Move to the rear!"
The driver on the bus
Goes "Move to the rear!"
All over town!

**The people on the bus
Go up and down,**
(and so on)

**The babies on the bus
Go "Wah! Wah! Wah!"**
(and so on)

**The mothers on the bus
Go "Shh, shh, shh,"**
(and so on)

(You can add other verses, too. Try "money goes clink," "wipers go swish," and "children go yak-kity-yak.")

WHERE IS THUMBKIN?

Where is Thumbkin?
Where is Thumbkin?

Here I am!

Here I am!

How are you today, sir?

Very well, I thank you.

Run away,

Run away.

(Repeat with all the fingers: Pointer, Tall Man,
Ring Man, and Pinkie.)

 # THE BEEHIVE

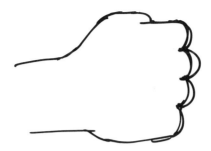

Here is the beehive.
Where are the bees?
Hidden away where nobody sees.
Watch as they come out of their hive—

One,   Two,   Three,   Four,   Five!

They're alive!
BZZZZ!

FIVE LITTLE MONKEYS

Five little monkeys
Jumping on the bed.

One fell off
And bumped his head.

Mama called the doctor,
And the doctor said,

shake
finger

"That's what you get
For jumping on the bed!"

Four little monkeys . . .
(and so on)

Three little monkeys . . .
(and so on)

Two little monkeys . . .
(and so on)

**One little monkey
Jumping on the bed.
He fell off
And bumped his head.
Mama called the doctor,
And the doctor said,
"No more monkeys
Jumping on the bed!"**

TEN FAT PEAS

Ten fat peas in a peapod pressed.

One grew. . . . Two grew. So did all the rest.

clap!

They grew and grew And did not stop Until one day
The pod went POP!

THE GRASSHOPPER

There was a little grasshopper

Who was always on the jump.

And because he never looked ahead,
He always got a bump.

IF YOU'RE HAPPY AND YOU KNOW IT

CLAP
TWICE
AFTER
SINGING
WORDS

If you're happy and you know it,
Clap your hands.

CLAP
TWICE

If you're happy and you know it,
Clap your hands.

CLAP
TWICE

If you're happy and you know it,
And you really want to show it,
If you're happy and you know it,
Clap your hands.

(Continue with other actions, such as stamp your
feet, touch your knees, nod your head, say
"Achoo!")

THE PEANUT SONG

Oh, a peanut sat
On a railroad track,

His heart was all a-flutter.

Along came the five-fifteen,

Uh-oh, peanut butter!

WHOOPS, JOHNNY!

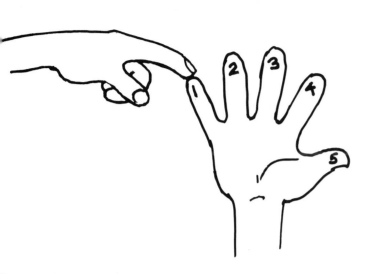

Johnny,

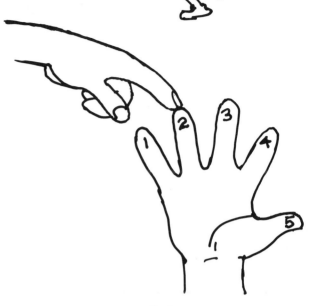

Johnny,

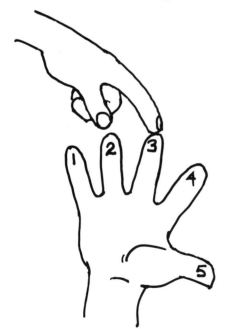

Johnny,

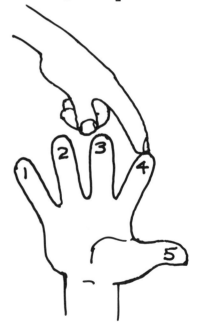

Johnny,

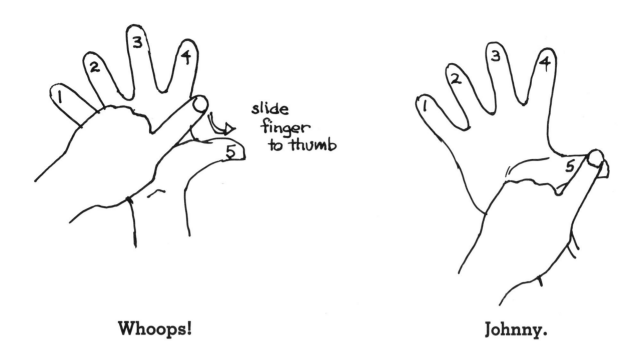

slide
finger
to thumb

Whoops!

Johnny.

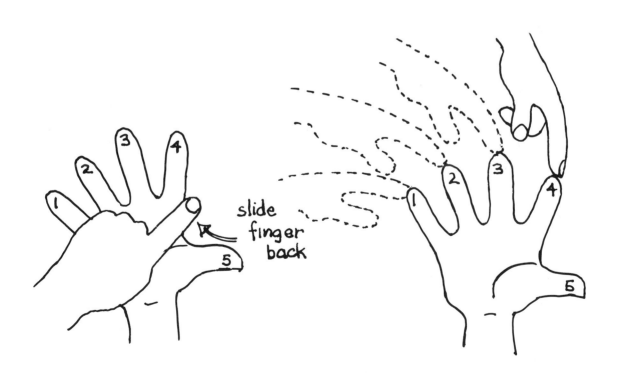

slide
finger
back

Whoops!

Johnny, Johnny, Johnny, Johnny.

THIS OLD MAN

This old man, he played one.

He played knick-knack
On his thumb.

With a knick-knack,

Paddy-whack,

Give your dog a bone.

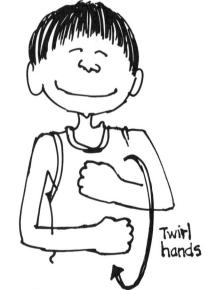

This old man came
Rolling home.

2nd Verse:

This old man, he played two.
He played knick-knack
On his shoe.

(and so on)

TOUCH SHOE

3rd Verse: "three" . . . "knee"

TOUCH KNEE

PRETEND TO KNOCK

4th Verse: "four" . . . "door"

5th Verse: "five" . . . "hive"

TAP FIST

6th Verse: "six" . . . "sticks"

TAP INDEX FINGERS TOGETHER

7th Verse: "seven" . . . "up to heaven"

POINT UP

TAP HAND

8th Verse: "eight" . . . "gate"

9th Verse: "nine" . . . "spine"

TAP SPINE

10th Verse: "ten" . . . "once again"

CLAP HANDS

TWO FAT GENTLEMEN

Two fat gentlemen
Met in a glen,

Bend one   Bend the other

Bowed most politely,
Bowed once again.

Bend both

How do you do? How do you do?
And how do you do again?

(Repeat with "two thin ladies" [index fingers]; "two
tall policemen" [middle fingers]; "two happy
schoolchildren" [ring fingers]; "two little babies"
[pinkies].)

CHOOK-CHOOK-CHOOK

Chook, chook, chook-chook-chook.
Good morning, Mrs. Hen.
How many children have you got?
Madam, I've got ten.

Four of them
Are yellow,

And four of them
Are brown,

And two of them
Are speckled red—
The nicest in the town!

THE ELEPHANT

The elephant goes like this and that.

He's oh, so big,
And he's oh, so fat.

He has no fingers,
And he has no toes,

But goodness gracious,
What a nose!

BIRTHDAY CAKE

Ten candles on a birthday cake,

All lit up for me.

I'll make a wish and blow them out.

Blow and bend fingers down

Watch and you will see.
Whhh!

ON MY HEAD

On my head my hands I place.

On my shoulders,

On my face,

On my hips,

And at my side,

Then behind me they will hide.

**I will hold them up so high,
Quickly make my fingers fly,**

Hold them out in front of me,

**Swiftly clap them—
One, two, three.**

TEN IN THE BED

There were ten in the bed,

And the little one said,
"Roll over! Roll over!"

So they all rolled over,
And one fell out.

There were nine in the bed,
(and so on)

There were eight in the bed. . . .

There were seven in the bed. . . .

There were six in the bed. . . .

There were five in the bed. . . .

There were four in the bed. . . .

There were three in the bed. . . .

There were two in the bed. . . .

There was one in the bed,
And the little one said,
"Good night!"

MUSICAL ARRANGEMENTS

SIX LITTLE DUCKS
(see pages 10-11)

Six lit - tle ducks That I once knew. Fat ducks, skin-ny ducks,
Down to the riv - er They would go, Wib-ble-wob-ble, wib-ble-wob-ble,

Fair ducks, too.} But the one lit - tle duck With a feath-er on his back,
To and fro. }

He led the oth-ers with a quack, quack, quack. Quack, quack, quack.

Quack, quack, quack. He led the oth-ers with a quack, quack, quack!

OPEN, SHUT THEM

(see pages 12-13)

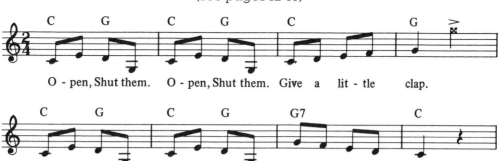

O - pen, Shut them. O - pen, Shut them. Give a lit - tle clap.

O - pen, Shut them. O - pen, Shut them. Place them in your lap.

Creep them, creep them. Creep them, creep them Right up to your chin.

O - pen wide your lit - tle mouth, But do not let them in.

I'M A LITTLE TEAPOT

(see page 20)

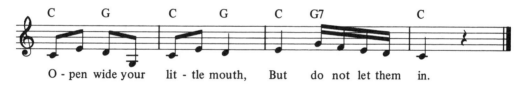

I'm a lit - tle tea - pot, Short and stout.

Here is my han - dle, Here is my spout. When I get all steamed up,

Hear me shout, "Tip me o - ver and pour me out!"

BLUEBIRDS

(see page 22)

Two lit - tle blue - birds Sit - ting on a hill,

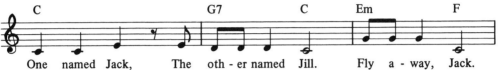

One named Jack, The oth - er named Jill. Fly a - way, Jack.

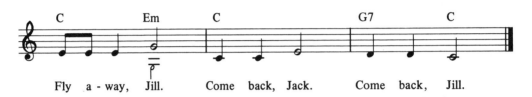

Fly a - way, Jill. Come back, Jack. Come back, Jill.

THE EENTSY, WEENTSY SPIDER

(see page 25)

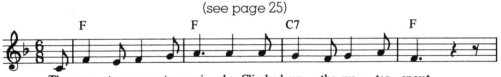

The een - tsy, ween - tsy spi - der Climbed up the wa - ter - spout.

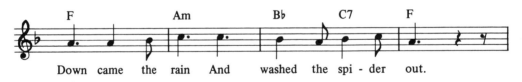

Down came the rain And washed the spi - der out.

Out came the sun And dried up all the rain. And the

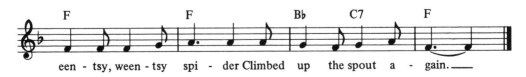

een - tsy, ween - tsy spi - der Climbed up the spout a - gain. ___

THE HAMMER SONG
(see pages 30-31)

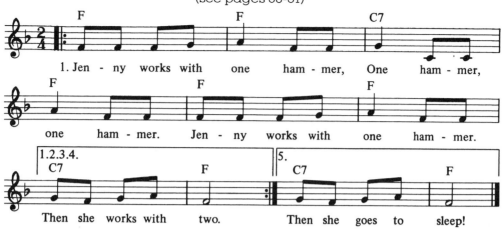

2. Jenny works with two hammers, Two hammers, two hammers.
Jenny works with two hammers. Then she works with three.

3. Jenny works with three hammers, Three hammers, three hammers.
Jenny works with three hammers. Then she works with four.

4. Jenny works with four hammers, Four hammers, four hammers.
Jenny works with four hammers. Then she works with five.

5. Jenny works with five hammers, Five hammers, five hammers.
Jenny works with five hammers. Then she goes to sleep!

THE WHEELS ON THE BUS
(see pages 34-35)

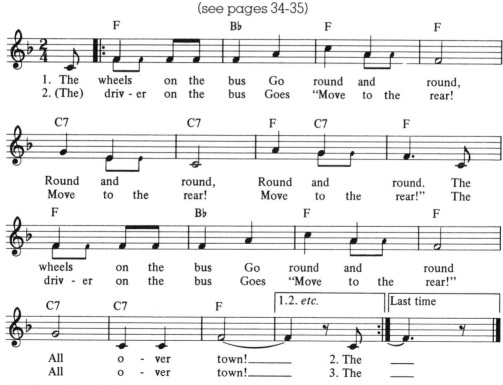

3. The people on the bus Go up and down, (etc.)
4. The babies on the bus Go "Wah! Wah! Wah!" (etc.)
5. The mothers on the bus Go "Shh, shh, shh," (etc.)

Note: You can add other verses, too.
Try, "money goes clink," "wipers go swish,"
and "children go yakkity-yak."

WHERE IS THUMBKIN?

(see page 36)

Where is Thumb - kin? Where is Thumb - kin?

Here I am! Here I am! How are you to - day, sir?

Ver - y well, I thank you. Run a - way, Run a - way.

(Repeat with all the fingers: Pointer, Tall Man, Ring Man, and Pinkie.)

IF YOU'RE HAPPY AND YOU KNOW IT

(see page 42)

If you're hap - py and you know it, Clap your hands. If you're

hap - py and you know it, Clap your hands. If you're

hap - py and you know it, And you real - ly want to show it, If you're

hap - py and you know it, Clap your hands.

(Continue with other actions, such as stamp your feet, nod your head, say "Achoo!")

THE PEANUT SONG

(see page 43)

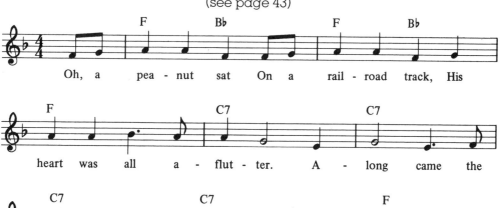

Oh, a pea - nut sat On a rail - road track, His

heart was all a - flut - ter. A - long came the

five - fif - teen, Uh - oh, pea - nut but - ter!

THIS OLD MAN

(see pages 46-47)

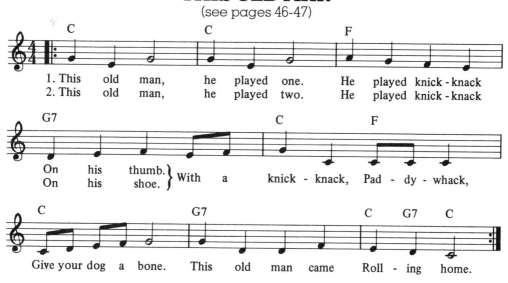

1. This old man, he played one. He played knick - knack
2. This old man, he played two. He played knick - knack

On his thumb.
On his shoe. } With a knick - knack, Pad - dy - whack,

Give your dog a bone. This old man came Roll - ing home.

ADDITIONAL VERSES:

3rd verse: "three" . . . "knee"   7th verse: "seven" . . . "up to heaven"
4th verse: "four" . . . "door"   8th verse: "eight" . . . "gate"
5th verse: "five" . . . "hive"   9th verse: "nine" . . . "spine"
6th verse: "six" . . . "sticks"   10th verse: "ten" . . . "once again"

TEN IN THE BED

(see pages 54-55)

There were ten in the bed, And the lit-tle one said, "Roll

(Repeat through "two in the bed,")

o - ver! Roll o - ver!" So they all rolled o - ver, And

one fell out. There were nine* in the bed, And the

(Repeat 7 times)

lit - tle one said, "Roll o - ver! Roll o - ver!" So they

(Last time only)

all rolled o - ver, And one fell out. There was

one in the bed, And the lit - tle one said, *(spoken)* "Good night!"

*Eight in the bed, etc.
Continue until "two in the bed,"
then end with "Last time only" section.

WHY DID THE CHICKEN CROSS THE ROAD?

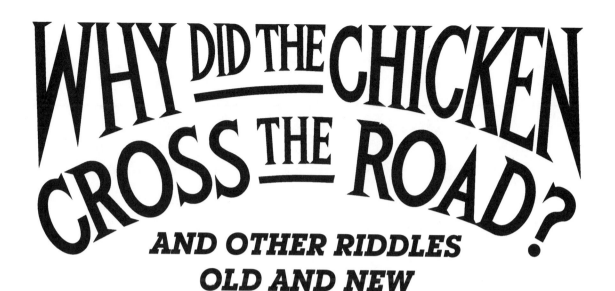

WHY DID THE CHICKEN CROSS THE ROAD?

AND OTHER RIDDLES OLD AND NEW

COMPILED BY

JOANNA COLE

AND

STEPHANIE CALMENSON

ILLUSTRATED BY

ALAN TIEGREEN

CONTENTS

ABOUT RIDDLES

I have an apple I cannot cut,
A blanket I cannot fold,
And so much money I cannot count it.

This is a riddle that was told long, long ago. The first riddles, say folklorists, go far back in human history. They were not necessarily funny. Rather, they were a way of looking at the world. They showed how two things that seem different on the surface are actually alike in some way. Many were about nature and the universe, and often they were more like poems than jokes.

The answer to the riddle above is: the moon, which is round like an apple; the sky, which is large and flat like a blanket; and the stars, which are scattered through the heavens like sparkling coins.

Other old riddles were matters of life and death. In the mythology of ancient Greece, a dragonlike creature called the Sphinx sat outside the city of Thebes and asked this riddle of everyone who passed:

What walks on four legs in the morning,
two legs at noon, and three legs at night?

Those who couldn't answer were killed by the Sphinx. Finally a man named Oedipus solved the riddle and destroyed the Sphinx. The answer he gave was: man, who crawls on all fours as a baby, walks on two feet as a man, and uses a cane in old age.

Riddles have changed a lot over the years. Now they are told mostly to amuse. The humor comes from playing with language, from taking advantage of the fact that one word often has two or more meanings. Your life may never depend on knowing the answers to the riddles in this book, but we hope they'll make you laugh.

Here is a riddle we'd like to close with:

Why did the pig keep turning around when he read this introduction?

He was looking for the end.

And here it is. . .

The End

WHY DID THE JELLY ROLL?
Sink your teeth into these funny food riddles.

What did the astronaut cook in his skillet?
Unidentified frying objects.

Why did the jelly roll?
Because it saw the apple turnover.

What's the best thing to put into a chocolate cake?
Your teeth.

How do you make a hamburger roll?

Take it to the top of a hill and give it a push.

How do you make a hot dog stand?

Take away its chair.

How do you make a lemon drop?

Let go of it.

How do you make a strawberry shake?

Put it in the fridge.

How do you make an ice cream pop?

Stick a pin in it.

WHAT DO YOU CALL A BABY WHALE?

Here are some silly ways to describe things.

What do you call two bananas?

A pair of slippers.

What do you call a sick alligator?

An illigator.

What do you call a baby whale?

A little squirt.

What do you call a bee who hums very quietly?

A mumblebee.

What do you call a pony with a sore throat?

A little hoarse.

What do you call a freight train loaded with bubble gum?

A chew-chew train.

What do you call someone who carries an encyclopedia in his pocket?

Smarty-pants.

THE 2,000-POUND GORILLA
He thinks these animal riddles are funny.
So start laughing.

Which side of a chicken has the most feathers?
The outside.

What do you call a 2,000-pound gorilla?
Sir.

What dog says "meow"?
A police dog working undercover.

Where do sheep get their hair cut?

At the baa-baa shop.

What is the best way to keep a skunk from smelling?

Hold his nose.

What do you call a black-and-blue Tyrannosaurus rex?

A dino-sore.

What happened to the cat who swallowed a ball of yarn?

She had mittens.

MORE ANIMAL RIDDLES

How do you know carrots are good for your eyes?
You never see a rabbit wearing glasses.

What is the best way to catch a squirrel?
Climb up a tree and act like a nut.

Why is it hard to talk with a goat around?
He keeps butting in.

Why don't ducks tell jokes while they're flying?
They might quack up.

**Why does a mother kangaroo
hope it doesn't rain?**

She hates it when the children have to play inside.

What did the boy octopus say to the girl octopus?

I want to hold your hand, hand, hand, hand, hand, hand, hand, hand.

**There were ten cats in a boat and one jumped out.
How many were left?**

None. They were copycats.

STILL MORE ANIMALS!

What do rhinoceroses have that no other animal has?

Baby rhinoceroses.

How do you keep a bull from charging?

Take away his credit card.

What does a vet keep outside his front door?

A welcome mutt.

What do you call a cow who works for a gardener?

A lawn mooer.

Why are fish so smart?

Because they live in schools.

How do baby birds learn to fly?

They wing it.

Why do bees hum?

Because they can't remember the words.

What was the turtle doing on the highway?

About one mile an hour.

AND DON'T FORGET THE ELEPHANT RIDDLES

Who is beautiful
and gray and wears
glass slippers?

Cinderelephant.

Why do elephants paint their toenails red?

So they can hide in the strawberry patch.

Why did the elephant sit on the marshmallow?

To keep from falling into the cocoa.

**What time is it when
the elephant
sits on the park bench?**

Time to get a new bench.

**How can you tell if there's been an elephant in your
refrigerator?**

You can see his footprints in the butter.

**What's the difference between an elephant and a
grape?**

The grape is purple.

What is gray and has four legs and a trunk?

A mouse going on vacation. (Fooled you!)

SHERLOCK BONES

Do you have time for some spooky riddles?
Better check your witch watch.

What did Dracula say when he got a present?

"Fangs a lot."

Why did the teacher send Dracula, Jr., home from school?

He was coffin too much.

How did the monster count to one hundred?

On his fingers.

What skeleton was a famous detective?

Sherlock Bones.

What do they call a skeleton who won't get out of bed?

Lazybones.

What is a monster's favorite breakfast cereal?

Scream of wheat.

What is a ghost's favorite kind of music?

Haunting melodies.

How did the witch babies get switched at birth?

It was hard to tell witch was witch.

What did the mother ghoul say to her child when it was raining?

Don't forget your ghoul-ashes.

How is a Cyclops like a pig?

They both have one eye (i) in the middle.

Which monster is a practical joker?

Prankenstein.

POOCHED EGGS ON TOAST

When you cross one thing with another,
you never know what you'll end up with.

What do you get when you cross two dogs, two eggs, and a slice of bread?

Pooched eggs on toast.

What do you get when you cross an elephant with a peanut butter sandwich?

An elephant that sticks to the roof of your mouth or a peanut butter sandwich that never forgets.

What do you get when you cross a rhino with a computer?

A very large know-it-all.

What do you get when you cross a cocker spaniel, a poodle, and a rooster?

A cock-a-poodle-doo.

What do you get when you cross a plumber with a jeweler?

A ring around the bathtub.

What do you get when you cross a cat with a laughing hyena?

A giggle puss.

What do you get when you cross a cat with a lemon?

A sour puss.

What do you get when you cross a hippo with a blackbird?

A lot of broken telephone poles.

What do you get when you cross a parrot with a tiger?

I don't know, but you'd better listen when it talks.

WHAT BOW CAN'T BE TIED?

Things are not always what they seem.

What kind of coat won't keep you warm?

A coat of paint.

What pool is no good for swimming?

A car pool.

What bow can't be tied?

A rainbow.

Which pen won't write?

A pigpen.

When is a door not a door?

When it's ajar.

When is a plane not a plane?

When it's aloft.

When is a bicycle not a bicycle?

When it turns into a driveway.

OLDIES AND NEWIES

Here are some of the oldest, best-known riddles in America, along with some modern versions.

The Fireman's Red Suspenders

The Oldie

Why does the fireman wear red suspenders?

To keep his pants up.

A Newie

Why does the fireman wear blue suspenders?

Because his red ones are in the wash.

Black, White, and Red

The Oldie

What's black and white and red all over?

A newspaper. (Read all over—get it?)

Some Newies

What's black and white and red all over?

A blushing zebra.

What's black and white and red all over?

A sunburned penguin.

MORE OLDIES AND NEWIES

Four Wheels and Flies

The Oldie

What has four legs and flies?

A horse in the summertime.

Some Newies

What has four wheels and flies?

A garbage truck.

What has eight wheels and flies?

A bird on roller skates.

The Chicken and the Road

The Oldie

Why did the chicken cross the road?

To get to the other side.

Some Newies

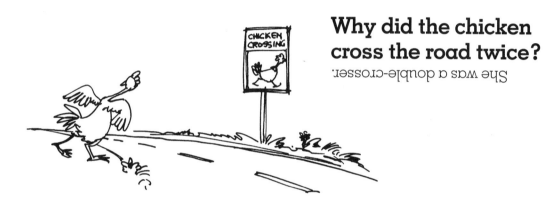

Why did the chicken cross the road twice?

She was a double-crosser.

Why did the turkey cross the road?

It was the chicken's day off.

WHAT DID DELAWARE?

Is geography funny? Try these riddles and see.

What did Delaware?

She wore her New Jersey.

What did Idaho?

She hoed her Maryland.

What did Tennessee?

She saw what Arkansas.

What state has four eyes but can't see?

Mississippi.

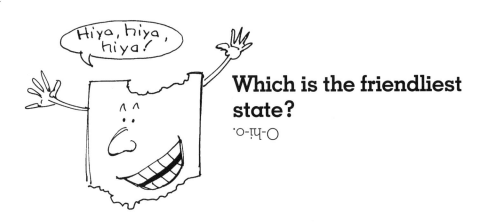

Hiya, hiya, hiya!

Which is the friendliest state?

O-hi-o.

If the green house is on the right side of the road and the red house is on the left side of the road, where is the white house?

In Washington, D.C.

Who should you call when you find Chicago, Ill?

Baltimore, MD.

Can you name the capital of every state in the union in less than fifteen seconds?

Yes, Washington, D.C.

Where do cows go on vacation?

Moo York.

WHY DID THE COMPUTER GO TO THE DOCTOR?

These doctor riddles will have you in stitches.

Why do surgeons wear masks?

So no one will recognize them if they make a mistake.

How did the psychiatrist help the confused pretzel?

She straightened it out.

Why did the boy bring a candy bar to the dentist?

He wanted a chocolate filling.

Why did the clock go to the doctor?

Because it felt run-down.

Why did the umbrella go to the doctor?

It was under the weather.

Why did the computer go to the doctor?

It thought it had a terminal illness.

TELL ME, DOCTOR...

How do you avoid illnesses caused by biting insects?

Don't bite any.

How do you keep from getting a pain in the eye when drinking chocolate milk?

Always take the spoon out of the glass.

How do you keep from getting corns on your toes?

Try planting beans instead.

WHY DID THE SILLY-BILLY SIT ON THE CLOCK?

Nothing is sillier
than a silly-billy riddle.

**Why did the silly-billy throw a stick
of butter out the window?**

He wanted to see a butterfly.

**Why did the silly-billy throw a
glass of water out the window?**

He wanted to see a waterfall.

**Why did the silly-billy sit
on the clock?**

He wanted to be on time.

Why did the silly-billy sit on the television set?

He wanted to be on TV.

Why did the silly-billy tiptoe past the medicine cabinet?

He didn't want to wake the sleeping pills.

YUK-
YUK!

Why did the silly-billy tell jokes to his stomach?

He wanted to hear belly laughs.

What showed up when the silly-billy had his head x-rayed?

Nothing.

WORSE AND WORSE

Complaining has never been so funny.

What is worse than a giraffe with a sore throat?

A centipede with sore feet.

What is worse than a centipede with sore feet?

A turtle with claustrophobia.

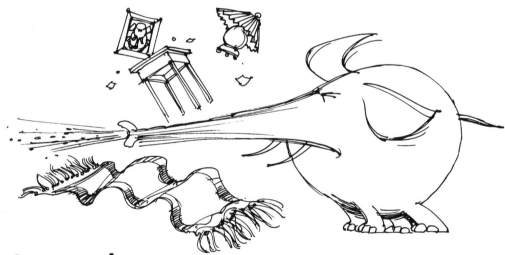

What is worse than a turtle with claustrophobia?

An elephant with hay fever.

WHAT TIME IS IT?
Oh, about five to funny.

What time is it when five grizzly bears are chasing you?
Five after one.

What time is it when you have a toothache?
Tooth-hurty.

What time was it when the baseball team evened the score?
Five to five.

What time is the same spelled backward or forward?
Noon.

Why should you never tell a secret near a clock?
Because time will tell.

A...B...C

There are more letters
in these riddles than there are
in the whole post office.

How many letters are there in the alphabet?

Eleven. T-H-E A-L-P-H-A-B-E-T.

What letters contain nothing?

M-T.

What starts with *T,* ends with *T,* and is filled with *T*?

A teapot.

If Washington went to Washington wearing white woollies while Washington's wife waited in Wilmington, how many *W*'s are there in all?

"There are no W's in "all.""

What ten-letter word starts with *G-A-S*?

Automobile.

MORE LETTER RIDDLES

What word begins with *E*, ends with *E*, and sounds as if it has only one letter in it?

Eye (I).

Spell *we* using two letters other than *W* or *E*.

U and I.

What five-letter word has six left when you take away two letters?

Sixty.

Why is *B* such a hot letter?

It makes oil boil.

Why is honey so scarce in Boston?

Because there is only one B in Boston.

How can you make a witch scratch?

Take away her W.

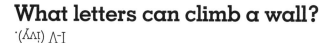

What letters can climb a wall?

I-V (ivy).

Which are the coldest two letters?

I-C (icy).

MOTHER GOOSE RIDDLES

Take a gander at these riddles from old nursery rhymes. Can you guess what they are about?

Humpty Dumpty sat on a wall.
Humpty Dumpty had a great fall.
All the king's horses
And all the king's men
Couldn't put Humpty together again.

An egg.

Little Nancy Etticoat
With a white petticoat,
And a red nose.
She has no feet or hands,
Yet the longer she stands,
The shorter she grows.

A lighted candle.

As I was going to St. Ives,
I met a man with seven wives.
Each wife had seven sacks,
Each sack had seven cats,
Each cat had seven kits.
Kits, cats, sacks, and wives,
How many were going to St. Ives?

One. (I was the only one going to St. Ives.)

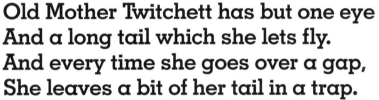

Old Mother Twitchett has but one eye
And a long tail which she lets fly.
And every time she goes over a gap,
She leaves a bit of her tail in a trap.

Needle and thread.

Thirty white horses
Upon a red hill;
Now they tramp,
Now they champ,
Now they stand still.

Teeth and tongue.

ONE, TWO, THREE
Count on these number riddles
to make you laugh.

Why is 6 afraid of 7?
Because 7 8 9.

If a person faints, what number should you bring him?
You should bring him 2.

How many feet in a yard?
It depends how many people are standing in it.

Why is 2 + 2 = 5 like your left foot?
It's not right.

How much is 5 Q plus 5 Q?

10 Q. (You're welcome.)

How many legs does a horse have?

Six. It has forelegs in the front and two legs in the back.

Why is two times ten the same as two times eleven?

Because two times ten equals twenty, and two times eleven equals twenty, too (twenty-two).

WHY DID THE BAKER QUIT HIS JOB?

Do these employees
take their work *seriously*?
What do you think?

How can you tell traffic cops are happy?

They whistle while they work.

Why did the baker quit his job?

He couldn't make enough dough.

How can you tell garbage collectors are sad?

They are often down in the dumps.

Which workers have the best hearing?

Engineers.

What does an attorney wear when he appears in court?

A lawsuit.

What did the author say when they asked her, "How's business?"

"Oh, it's all write."

Why did the mattress salesman get fired?

For lying down on the job.

When are cooks mean?

When they beat the eggs and whip the cream.

Why did the astronaut get the day off?

Because the moon was full.

WHAT DID THE PENCIL SAY TO THE PAPER?

Listen in on these silly conversations.

What did the strawberries say to the farmer?

"Stop picking on me!"

What did the mayonnaise say to the refrigerator?

"Close the door—I'm dressing."

What did the launchpad say to the rocket?

"Can I give you a lift?"

What did the pencil say to the paper?

"I dot my i on you."

What did the beaver say to the tree?

"It's been nice gnawing you."

What did the dirt say to the rain?

"Please stop, or my name will be mud."

What did the lamb say to his mother?

"Thank ewe."

What did one wall say to the other?

"Meet you at the corner."

What did one library book say to the other?

"Can I take you out?"

What did the mother broom say to the baby broom?

"Go to sweep, dear."

WHAT COLOR WAS WASHINGTON'S WHITE HORSE?

Watch out for these tricky riddles!

Antidisestablishmentarianism is the longest word in the English language. How do you spell it?

I-T.

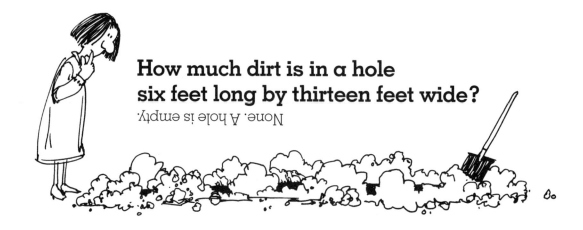

How much dirt is in a hole six feet long by thirteen feet wide?

None. A hole is empty.

Which weighs more: a pound of lead or a pound of feathers?

They both weigh a pound.

What color was Washington's white horse?

White.

How many animals did Moses take on the ark?

Moses didn't take any animals on the ark. Noah did.

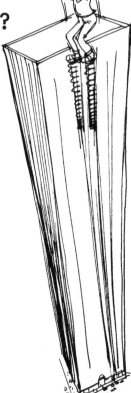

Who can jump higher than a tall building?

Anyone can. Tall buildings can't jump.

If a rooster laid a white egg and a brown egg, what kinds of chicks would hatch?

None. Roosters don't lay eggs.

Do you say, "Eight and seven *is* thirteen," or "Eight and seven *are* thirteen"?

Neither. Eight and seven equal fifteen.

MORE TRICKY ONES

Why was George Washington buried at Mount Vernon?

Because he was dead.

Who is buried in Grant's tomb?

Ulysses S. Grant.

How many acorns grow on the average pine tree?

None. Pine trees don't have acorns.

Is it better to write on a full stomach or an empty stomach?

It's better to write on paper.

Which would you rather have, an old ten-dollar bill or a new one?

I'd rather have any ten-dollar bill than a new one-dollar bill.

Six children, four adults, and two dogs shared one small umbrella. Who got wet?

No one. It wasn't raining.

How many jelly beans can you put in an empty jelly-bean jar?

Only one. After that the jar isn't empty anymore.

When can you knock over a full glass and not spill any water?

When the glass is full of milk.

If it takes thirteen men eleven days to dig a hole, how long will it take seven men to dig half a hole?

There is no such thing as half a hole.

WHAT'S THE DIFFERENCE...?
Find out in these riddles.

What's the difference between a prizefighter and a man with a cold?

One knows his blows and the other blows his nose.

What's the difference between a counterfeit dollar and a crazy rabbit?

One is bad money and the other is a mad bunny.

What's the difference between a butcher and a light sleeper?

One weighs a steak and the other stays awake.

What's the difference between a teacher and a railway engineer?

One trains the mind and the other minds the train.

What's the difference between a jail warden and a jeweler?

One watches cells and the other sells watches.

What's the difference between a rain gutter and a clumsy outfielder?

One catches drops and the other drops catches.

FLIP, FLOP, FLEEZY

Rhyming riddles were popular in olden days.
See if you can guess these.

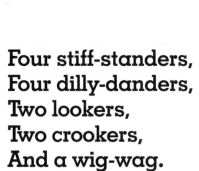

Flip, flop, fleezy,
Slippery, wet, and greasy.
When it's out,
It flops about.
Flip, flop, fleezy.

Fish.

Four stiff-standers,
Four dilly-danders,
Two lookers,
Two crookers,
And a wig-wag.

Cow.

When it flares up, it does a lot of good.
But when it dies, it's just paper or wood.

Match.

Very nice, very neat,
Has teeth, but cannot eat.

Comb.

Runs all day,
But never runs away.

Clock.

Riddle cum, riddle cum ruckup,
What fell down and stuck up?

Fork.

It wasn't my sister nor my brother,
But still was the child of my father and mother.
Who was it?

Myself.

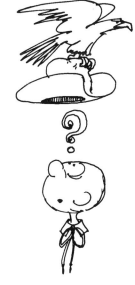

Riddle me, riddle me, what is that
Over the head and under the hat?

Hair.

WHAT GOES Z-Z-U-B, Z-Z-U-B?

Do you hear a strange sound?
Find out what is making it in these noisy riddles!

What goes *abcdefghijklmnopqrstuvwxyz slurp*?

Someone eating alphabet soup.

What goes *99 thump, 99 thump, 99 thump. . .*?

A centipede with a wooden leg.

What goes *z-z-u-b, z-z-u-b*?

A bee flying backward.

What goes *hoe, hoe, hoe*?

A farmer laughing.

DID YOU HEAR THE ONE ABOUT...?

You haven't heard yet?
Well, here's your chance.

Did you hear the one about the memory contest?

Yes, but I forgot.

Did you hear the one about the skunk?

It stank.

Did you hear the one about the butter?

Please don't spread it around.

Did you hear the one about the pencil?

Yes, I wrote it down.

Did you hear the one about the elevator?

It had its ups and downs.

Did you hear the one about the dinosaur egg?

It cracked me up in a big way.

HOW DID THE TREE SAY GOOD-BYE?
Here are a few fond farewells.

How did the ocean say good-bye?
It waved.

How did the shopper say good-bye?
"Buy-buy."

How did the tree say good-bye?

"Gotta leave."

How did the needle and thread say good-bye?

"Sew long."

How did the eye doctor say good-bye?

How do you say
good-bye to a friend?

Take three letters away,
and that is the end.

SIX SICK SHEEP

SIX SICK SHEEP

101 TONGUE TWISTERS

COMPILED BY
JOANNA COLE
AND
STEPHANIE CALMENSON

ILLUSTRATED BY
ALAN TIEGREEN

CONTENTS

HOW TONGUE TWISTERS BEGAN
A TONGUE-IN-CHEEK STORY

Once upon a time a king had to give a speech. His tongue got all tangled up. He was trying to say, "Trust train track taxes to triple today." Instead he said, "Trunst train tack trapples to tickle today." The people laughed. So did the king. He forgot the taxes, but everyone remembered the twister. People have been twisting their tongues ever since.

If you believe this story, you're ready for the wild tongue twisters in this book.

Twist a twister,
Twist your tongue-ster.
These are fun
For every youngster!

Youngsters, oldsters,
Join the fun—
Twist some twisters,
Trick your tongue!

GETTING STARTED

Warm up your tongue with these twisters.

Nat's knapsack strap snapped.

Sam's sock shop stocks short spotted socks.

Rubber baby buggy bumpers.

Andy ran to the Andes from the Indies in his undies.

Shirley sewed Sly's shirt shut.

Pick up six pick-up sticks quickly.

SHEEPISH SHAYINGS...
ER, WE MEAN SHEEPISH *SAYINGS*

Six sick sheep.
The sixth sick sheep is the sheik's sixth sheep.

Sheep shouldn't sleep in a shack.
Sheep should sleep in a shed.

Say, does this sheet shop serve sheep, sir?

Sam shaved seven shy sheep.
Seven shaved sheep shivered shyly.

Seasick sheep sail slowly.

NIGHT, NIGHT!

You've no need to light a night-light
On a light night like tonight.
For a night-light's light's a slight light,
And tonight's a night that's light.
When a night's light, like tonight's light,
It is really not quite right
To light night-lights with their slight lights
On a light night like tonight.

"Night, night," said the knight to the knight one night.

Nine nice night nurses nursing nicely.

FAST FOOD

See how fast you can say these tongue twisters about food. Ready, set, go!

Fred's friend Fran flips fine flapjacks fast.

A proper copper coffeepot.

Sue chews string cheese.

Bruce bought bad brown bran bread.

Four famished French fishermen frying flying fish.

OH, SAY CAN YOU SAY?

All these twisters have the *S* sound. See if you can say 'em.

Say this sharply, say this sweetly,
Say this shortly, say this softly.
Say this sixteen times in succession.

Six slim, slick saplings.

She says she shall sew a sheet.

Sure the ship's shipshape, sir.

SHORT TAKES

Say these two-word twisters three times fast.
They may be short, but they're not easy.

Preshrunk shirts.

Lemon liniment.

Truly rural.

Mixed biscuits.

Soldiers' shoulders.

Peggy Babcock.

Greek grapes.

Aluminum linoleum.

STELLA'S SNEAKERS
A Tongue Twister Story

Every word in this story begins with the letter *S*. Try reading it aloud without tripping over your tongue.

Someone sold Stella super striped sneakers. Stella stood. Stella stepped. Stella slipped.

"Shucks!" shrieked Stella. Sam's silver steam shovel scooped Stella skyward.

Star-struck Stella sideswiped Shelly's shiny space station. "Stay, Stella. Sip some sweet soda," said Shelly.

"Sure," said Stella. Stella sipped. Stella stepped. Stella slipped. She slipped south. Sam's steam shovel scooped Stella safely.

Sam soon saw Stella's sign: Sale—Super Slippery Striped Sneakers.

COULD-A, WOULD-A, SHOULD-A

I would if I could.
If I couldn't, how could I?
I couldn't if I couldn't, could I?
If you couldn't, you couldn't, could you?

Little Willie wouldn't whistle on his wooden whistle, would he?

Shelly shouldn't shake saltshakers, should she?

PETER PIPER'S PATTERN

Some tongue twisters follow a familiar pattern. Take a sentence. Turn the sentence into a question. Then make another question, the first part beginning with "If" and the second part beginning with "Where." Here are two examples. Can you make up some others?

Peter Piper picked a peck of pickled peppers.
Did Peter Piper pick a peck of pickled peppers?
If Peter Piper picked a peck of pickled peppers,
Where's the peck of pickled peppers Peter Piper picked?

Billy Button bought a buttered biscuit.
Did Billy Button buy a buttered biscuit?
If Billy Button bought a buttered biscuit,
Where's the buttered biscuit Billy Button bought?

OVER AND OVER AND OVER

These twisters repeat one word many times. What makes them extra-fun is that the same word has two meanings.

I have a can opener that can open any can that any can opener that can open any can can open. If you will give me a can that any can opener that can open any can can open, I will open that can that any can opener that can open any can can open with my can opener that can open any can that any can opener that can open any can can open.

I thought a thought.
But the thought I thought
wasn't the thought
I thought I thought.
If the thought I thought
I thought had been
the thought I thought,
I wouldn't have
thought so much.

Of all the felt I ever felt, I never felt
a piece of felt that felt the same
as that felt felt when I first felt felt.

The undertaker undertook to undertake an undertaking. The undertaking that the undertaker undertook to undertake was the hardest undertaking the undertaker ever undertook to undertake.

If one doctor doctors another doctor, does the doctor
who doctors the doctor doctor the doctor the way the
doctor he is doctoring doctors? Or does he doctor the
doctor the way the doctor who doctors doctors?

SALLY AT THE SEASHORE

Sally sells seashells by the seashore.

She sells seashells on the seashell shore.
The seashells she sells are seashore shells,
Of that I'm sure.

She sells seashells by the seashore.
She hopes she will sell all her seashells soon.

If neither he sells seashells
Nor she sells seashells,
Who shall sell seashells?
Shall seashells be sold?

A TONGUE TWISTER GAME

For three or more players.

One player, the leader, reads the first tongue twister. Each of the other players repeats that twister in turn. Then the leader reads the second twister. Each player must say the first *and* second twisters. The game goes on adding one twister at a time. The winner is the one who can say all ten twisters correctly.

One wise whistling wizard.

Two tooting tuba-tuners.

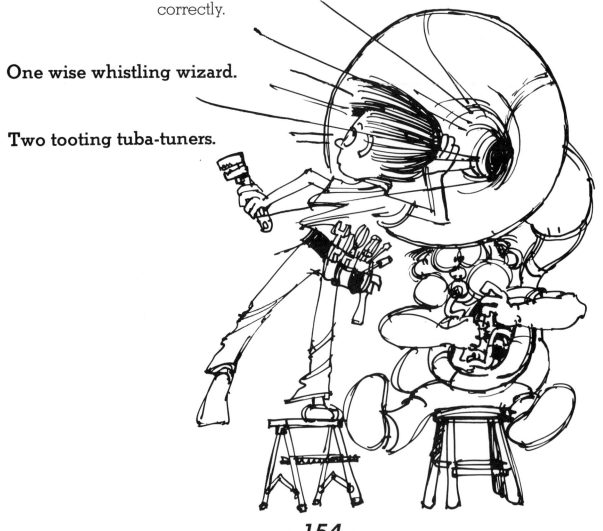

Three twirling tricky tree toads.

Four fresh French flamingos.

Five freezing fleeing foxes.

Six sharp sleepy sharks.

Seven short striped snakes.

Eight eager able eagles.

Nine itching inching inchworms.

Ten tiny timid tigers.

(Try making up your own twisters for this game.)

IMPRESS YOUR FRIENDS

Can you memorize a long tongue twister and recite it without making a mistake? Try some of these.

Mr. Inside went over to see Mr. Outside.
Mr. Inside stood outside and called to Mr. Outside inside.
Mr. Outside answered Mr. Inside from inside
And told Mr. Inside to come inside.
Mr. Inside said, "No," for Mr. Outside to come outside.
Mr. Outside and Mr. Inside argued from inside and outside
About going outside or coming inside.
Finally, Mr. Inside coaxed Mr. Outside to come outside,
And Mr. Outside coaxed Mr. Inside to go inside.
Then Mr. Inside was inside, and Mr. Outside was outside.
Were they satisfied or fit to be tied? You decide!

Say, did you say or did you not say
What I said you said?
For it is said that you said
That you did not say
What I said you said.
Now, if you say that you did not say
What I said you said,
Then what do you say you did say instead
Of what I said you said?

Betty Botter bought some butter.
"But," she said, "the butter's bitter.
If I put it in my batter,
It will make my batter bitter,
But a bit of better butter,
That would make my batter better."
So she bought a bit of butter
Better than her bitter butter,
And she put it in her batter,
And the batter was not bitter.
So t'was better Betty Botter
Bought a bit of better butter.

Mr. See owned a saw.
And Mr. Soar owned a seesaw.
Now See's saw sawed Soar's seesaw
Before Soar saw See,
Which made Soar sore.
Had Soar seen See's saw
Before See sawed Soar's seesaw,
See's saw would not have sawed
Soar's seesaw.
So See's saw sawed Soar's seesaw,
But it was sad to see Soar so sore
Just because See's saw sawed Soar's seesaw.

TRIPLE TWISTERS

Each of these twisters is made up of three words. Say them fast three times and see how you do.

Three free throws.

Ruth's red roof.

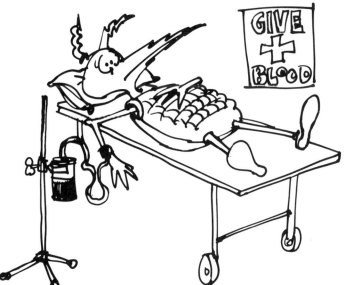

Blue bug's blood.

Please freeze cheese.

Supper at sixish.

Unique New York.

Fred's fruit float.

Plain plum bun.

Miss Matthew's myth.

Sixty sticky thumbs.

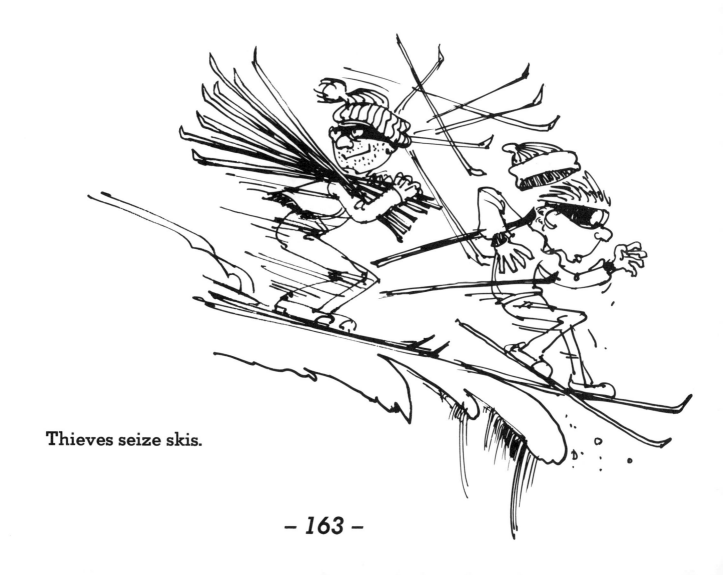

Thieves seize skis.

HE SAW, SHE SAW

I was looking back
To see if she was looking back
To see if I was looking back
To see if she was looking back at me.

I saw Esau kissing Kate,
And Kate saw I saw Esau,
And Esau saw that I saw Kate,
And Kate saw I saw Esau saw.

ANIMALS, ANIMALS

How much wood would a woodchuck chuck
If a woodchuck could chuck wood?
A woodchuck would chuck as much wood
As a woodchuck could chuck
If a woodchuck could chuck wood.

Five fat frogs fly past fast.
The fattest frog passes fastest.

Swan swam over the sea.
Swim, swan, swim!
Swan swam back again.
Well swum, swan!

A skunk sat on a stump.
The stump thunk the skunk stunk.
The skunk thunk the stump stunk.

ALPHABET GAME

You can play this game by yourself, simply making up a twister for each letter of the alphabet. For more players, the first player must make up a tongue twister for the letter *A*. The next player makes up one for *B*, and so on in turn.

Tips for making twisters: Think of sounds that confuse the tongue—such as *th* and *thr*, as in three thin thumbs; *f*, *fr*, and *fl*, as in fat flying frogs; or *s* and *sh*, as in she sells seashells.

A **Ask after Asta's asthma.**

B **Bessie bought Beth's beef broth.**

C **Clowns crown crabs and clams.**

D   Ducks, don't drive, dive!

E   Ethel's elegant elephant'll elevate Ethel.

...and so on, until *Z*.

T–TWISTERS

A twister of twists
Once twisted a twist,
And the twist that he twisted
Was a three-twisted twist.
Now in twisting this twist,
If a twist should untwist,
That twist that untwisted
Would untwist the twist.

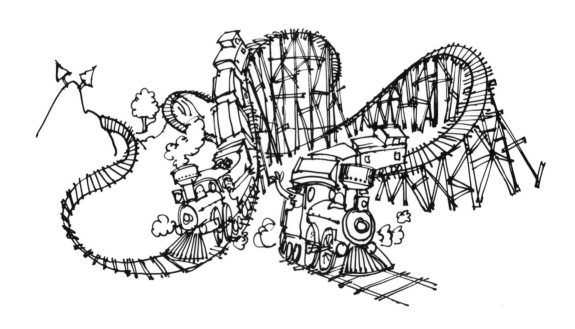

Two twin trains travel twisted tracks.

A tutor who tooted a flute
Tried to tutor two tooters to toot.
Said the two to their tutor,
"Is it harder to toot or
To tutor two tooters to toot?"

SAY-IT-AGAIN GAME

For two or more players.

Each player takes a turn saying a twister over and over again until he or she makes a mistake. The player who repeats the twister the most times is the winner.

You can use any tongue twister in this book, but the ones that follow are especially hard to say more than once.

Which wristwatch is the Swiss wristwatch?

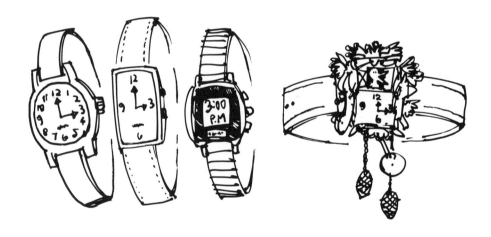

Red leather, yellow leather.

Double bubble gum bubbles double.

TWO TONGUE TWISTER POEMS

They twist *and* they rhyme!

An oyster met an oyster,
And they were oysters two;
Two oysters met two oysters,
And they were oysters, too.
Four oysters met a pint of milk,
And they were oyster stew!

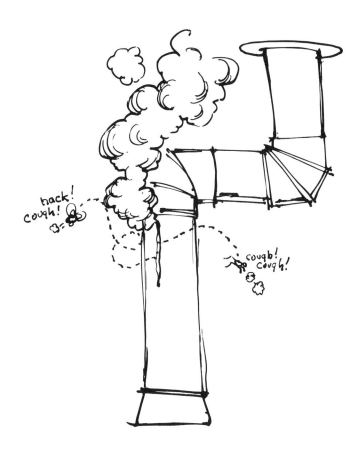

A flea and a fly flew up in a flue.
Said the flea, "Let us fly!"
Said the fly, "Let us flee!"
So they flew through a flaw in the flue.

FISHY TWISTS

I never smelled a smelt that smelled as bad as that smelt smelled.

I often sit and think
And fish and sit
And fish and think
And sit and fish
And think and wish
That I could get a cool drink!

WEATHER REPORT

Flee from fog to fight flu fast.

Lesser leather never weathered wetter weather better.

No snow shows like slow snow shows.

We shall surely see the sun shine soon.

OH, BROTHER!

Ben's brother's big black-backed bath brush broke.

A brother to his brother did utter,
"Go, my brother, and shut the shutter."
"The shutter's shut," the brother did utter.
"I cannot shut it any shutter."

OH, SISTER!

Sue's sister switched silk shoes.
Which silk shoes did Sue's sister switch?

This sis sits on thistles.

LAST ONE

Tip-top, tangle tongue,
Say this twister and you're done:
He who last laughs laughs last.

PAT-A-CAKE

PAT-A-CAKE
AND OTHER PLAY RHYMES

COMPILED BY
JOANNA COLE AND
STEPHANIE CALMENSON

ILLUSTRATED BY **ALAN TIEGREEN**

CONTENTS

PLAY RHYMES
FOR BABIES AND TODDLERS

Pat-a-cake, pat-a-cake, baker's man,
Bake me a cake as fast as you can.
Roll it and pat it and mark it with *B*,
And put it in the oven for Baby and me!

For many of us, "Pat-a-Cake" was the first game we learned, and so it was the first game we taught our own babies. It is just one of the many tried-and-true games babies love.

In this book, you will find games for every mood and time of day—tickling rhymes, dancing rhymes, toe-and-foot rhymes, finger-and-hand rhymes. It's fun to play "Pitty, Patty, Polt," for example, when you're drying Baby's feet after a bath. "Baby's Nap" is a soothing rhyme before bed. "Two Little Eyes" is a perfect mealtime rhyme. And "Trot Along to Boston" and other knee-riding rhymes are exciting anytime.

When playing with a baby, a little stimulation goes a long way. If your child seems less than eager to play a game, maybe he feels overwhelmed. Try it a different way. For instance, touch the baby softly instead of tickling him, or swing him gently on your ankle instead of bouncing him on your knee.

Even before a child can talk, she is learning language from listening to you. And before a child can walk, she is practicing the movements she will need later on. These simple games, which combine physical play with imaginative words, are perfect for developing babies and toddlers. And, best of all, they're fun!

PAT-A-CAKE

Pat-a-cake, pat-a-cake, baker's man,
Bake me a cake as fast as you can.

Roll it   and pat it   and mark it with *B*.

And put it in the oven for Baby and me.

THIS LITTLE COW

This little cow eats grass.

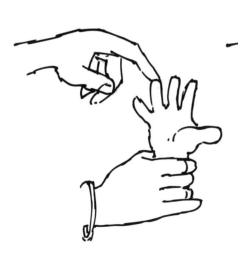

This little cow
eats hay.

This little cow
looks over the hedge.

This little cow
runs away.

And this BIG cow does nothing at all
But lie in the fields all day!
Let's chase her
        And chase her
                And chase her!

 **BABY'S NAP**

This is Baby ready for a nap.

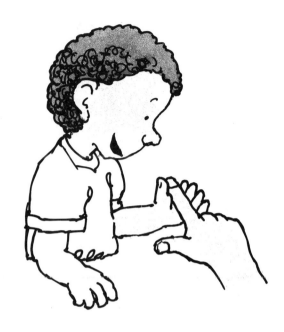

Lay Baby down in a loving lap.

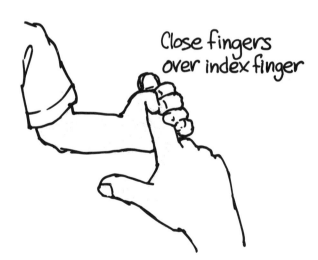

Close fingers over index finger

Cover Baby so he won't peep.

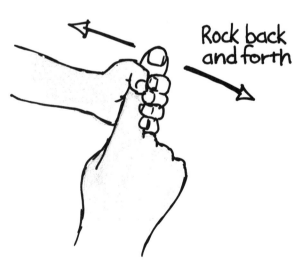

Rock back and forth

Rock Baby till he's fast asleep.

FOXY'S HOLE

Put your finger in Foxy's hole.
Foxy's not at home.

Foxy's at the back door,
Picking on a bone.

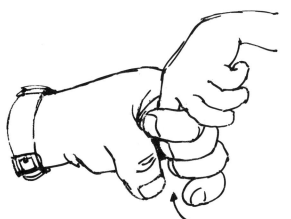

Gently "nip" Baby's finger
with your little finger

HERE IS BABY'S BALL

Here is Baby's ball,
Big and soft and round.

Here is Baby's hammer.
See how it can pound.

Here is Baby's trumpet,
Tootle-tootle-too.

Here is Baby's favorite game.
It's called Peek-a-Boo!

THESE ARE BABY'S FINGERS

These are Baby's fingers.

These are Baby's toes.

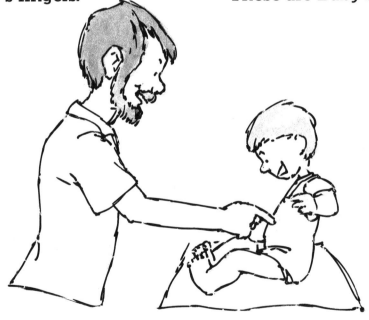

Gently circle belly button

This is Baby's tummy button.
Round and round it goes.

SEE MY TEN FINGERS

See my ten fingers dance and play.
Ten fingers dance for me today.

See my ten toes dance and play.
Ten toes dance for me today.

THIS LITTLE PIGGY

This little piggy went to market.

This little piggy
stayed home.

This little piggy
had roast beef.

This little piggy
had none.

And this little piggy cried,
Wee, wee, wee, wee,
All the way home.

WEE WIGGY, POKE PIGGY

Wee Wiggy,

Poke Piggy,

Tom Whistle,

John Gristle,

And old BIG GOBBLE,
Gobble, gobble!

LET'S GO TO THE WOOD

"Let's go to the wood," says this pig.
"What will we do?" says that pig.
"Look for my mother," says this pig.
"What will we do?" says that pig.
"Kiss her, kiss her, kiss her!" says this pig.

Touch toes
in same sequence
as in Wee Wiggy
on previous page

1 2 3 4 5

PITTY, PATTY, POLT

Pat soles of Baby's feet
in rhythm

Pitty, patty, polt.
Shoe the wild colt.
Here's a nail.
There's a nail.
Pitty, patty, polt!

SHOE THE LITTLE HORSE

Shoe the little horse.
Shoe the little mare.

But let the little colt
Run bare, bare, bare.

EYE WINKER, TOM TINKER

Gently touch eyelid

Eye winker,

Tom tinker,

nose smeller,

mouth eater,

chin chopper,

guzzle whopper!

TWO LITTLE EYES

Two little eyes to look around.

Two little ears to hear each sound.

One little nose to smell what's sweet.

One little mouth that likes to eat.

KNOCK AT THE DOOR

Knock at the door.

Peep in.

Lift up the latch.

Walk in!

HERE SITS FARMER GILES

Here sits Farmer Giles.

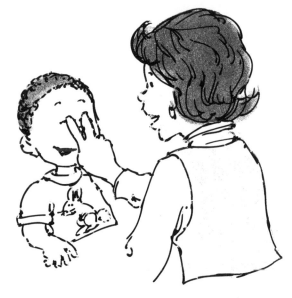

Here sit his two men.

Here sits the cockadoodle.

Here sits the hen.

Here sit the little chickens.

Here they run in.

Chin chopper,
Chin chopper,
Chin, chin, chin.

CHOP–A–NOSE DAY

My mother and your mother
Went over the way.

Said your mother to my mother,

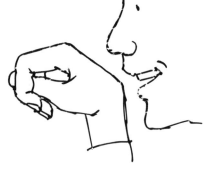

"It's chop-a-nose day!"

CREEPY MOUSE

Creepy mouse,
Creepy mouse,
All the way up

Creep fingers up
Baby's arm

To Baby's house!

Tickle neck

I'M GOING TO BORE A HOLE

Circle index finger above Baby

Make circles smaller

I'm going to bore a hole,
And I don't know where.

I think I'll bore a hole right...

Poke Baby gently

THERE!

THIS LITTLE TRAIN

This little train ran up the track.
It went *toot, toot,*
And then came back.

Run fingers
up one arm
and back down

Repeat with
other arm

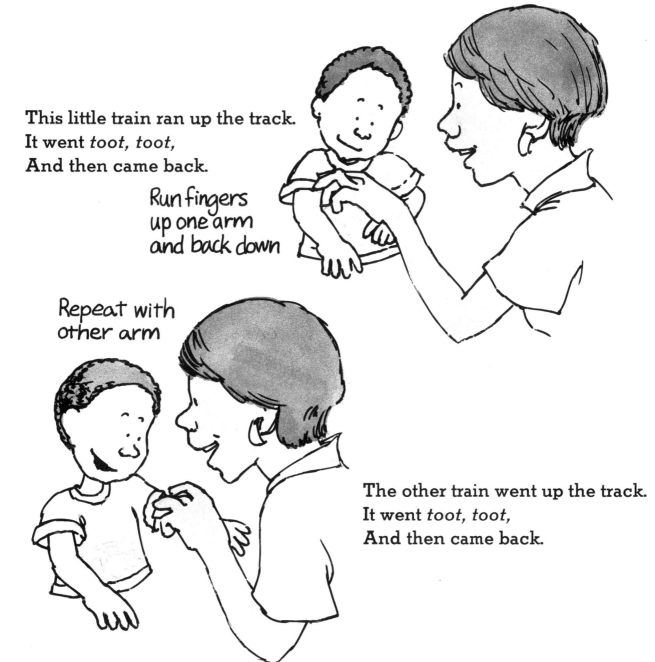

The other train went up the track.
It went *toot, toot,*
And then came back.

ROUND AND ROUND
THE GARDEN

Round and round the garden
Like a teddy bear.
One step, two step,

Tickle you under there!

RIDE A COCK HORSE
TO BANBURY CROSS

Ride a cock horse to Banbury Cross,
To see a fine lady upon a white horse.
Rings on her fingers,
And bells on her toes,
She shall have music
Wherever she goes.

GIDDYAP, HORSIE, TO THE FAIR

Giddyap, horsie, to the fair.
What'll we buy when we get there?
A penny apple and a penny pear.
Giddyap, horsie, to the fair.

THE DOG GOES TO DOVER

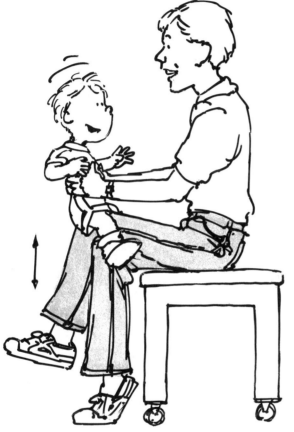

Leg over leg,
As the dog goes to Dover.
When he comes to a wall,

Jump! He goes over!

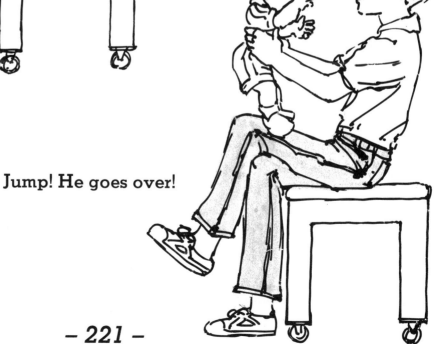

HERE WE GO UP, UP, UP

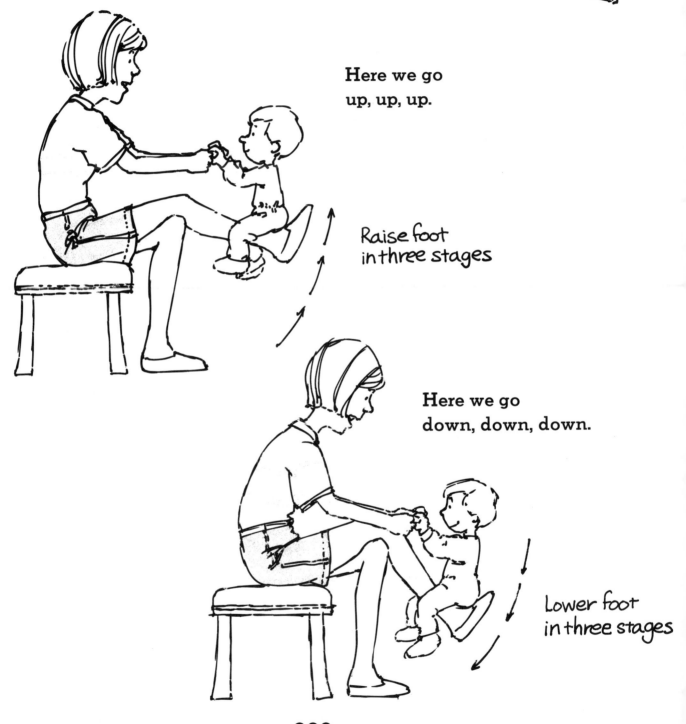

Here we go
up, up, up.

Raise foot
in three stages

Here we go
down, down, down.

Lower foot
in three stages

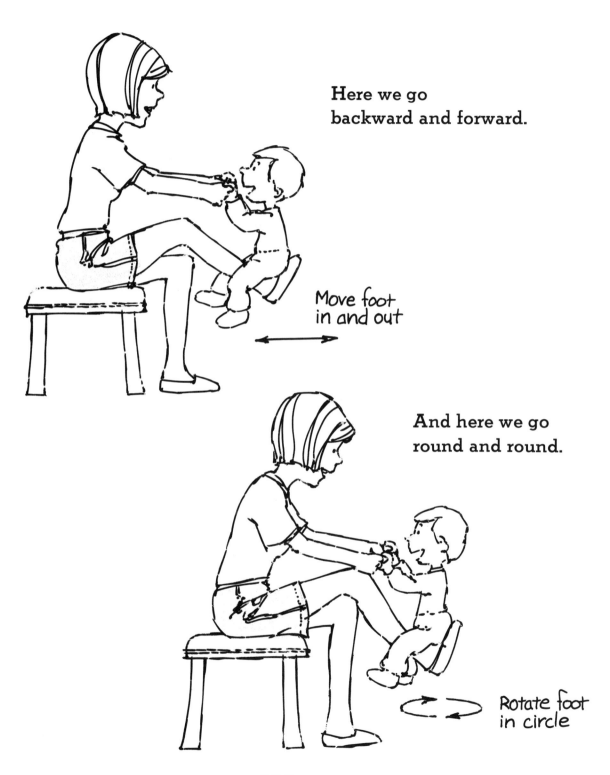

Here we go
backward and forward.

Move foot
in and out

And here we go
round and round.

Rotate foot
in circle

- 223 -

PONY GIRL or PONY BOY

Pony girl, pony girl,
Won't you be my pony girl?
Giddyap, giddyap, giddyap,

WHEE!

My pony girl!

TROT ALONG TO BOSTON

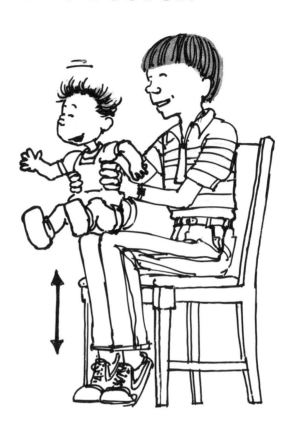

Trot along to Boston.
Trot along to Lynn.
Better watch out,

Or you'll fall in!

FATHER AND MOTHER
AND UNCLE JOHN

Father and Mother and Uncle John
Went to market, one by one.

Father fell off!   Mother fell off!

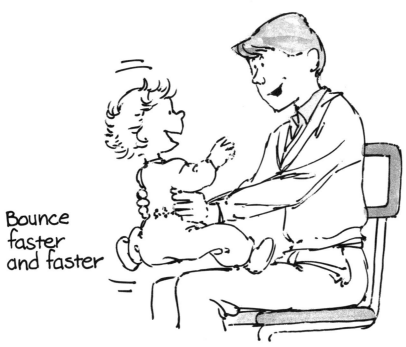

Bounce
faster
and faster

But Uncle John went on, and on,
And on, and on, and on.

RING AROUND THE ROSIE

Ring around the rosie.
Pocket full of posies.

Ashes, ashes,
We all fall down!

DANCE TO YOUR DADDY

Do a simple dance

Dance to your daddy,
My little Baby.
Dance to your daddy,
My little lamb.
You shall have a fishy
In a little dishy.
You shall have a fishy
When the boat comes in.